P9-DUV-647

BEAUTIFUL
BEADING

BEAUTIFUL BEADING

SARA WITHERS

Over 30 Original Designs for
Handmade Beads, Jewelry,
and Decorative Objects

Sterling Publishing Co., Inc.
New York

Library of Congress Cataloging-in-Publication Data Available

1 2 3 4 5 6 7 8 9 10

Published in 2002 by Sterling Publishing Co., Inc.
387 Park Avenue South, New York, N.Y. 10016
Distributed in Canada by Sterling Publishing
c/o Manda Group, One Atlantic Avenue, Suite 105
Toronto, Ontario, Canada M6K 3E7

Conceived and produced by Breslich & Foss Ltd., London

Printed and bound in Malaysia
All Rights Reserved

ISBN 0-8069-8945-9

Text: Sara Withers
Illustrations: Kate Simunek
Photography: Shona Wood
Project Management: Katy Lord
Design: Roger Daniels

contents

introduction

Right now the world seems to be full of beads. Designers of accessories, jewelry, and interiors are reveling in the richness of their colors, the diversity of their shapes, and the wide spectrum of techniques that can be applied to beads—wiring, threading, weaving, sticking, and embroidering. Beads have been valued for centuries, and can contribute to the understanding of our social and cultural history. *Beautiful Beading* aims to give you an enjoyment of beads, and demonstrate the techniques that you can use with them. You will learn to make beads from polymer clays, papier mâché, metal, and plastic. You won't just thread the beads, you will learn to weave them by hand and on a bead loom. You will wire them together, not just as jewelry but to create decorative pieces for the home. *Beautiful Beading* gives help on choosing beads, and guidance on which tools, threads, and findings you will need. All of the projects are designed to be inspirational, so that, if you wish to, you can adapt and alter them for your own needs.

When you have finished the book I hope that you will go on to create even more pieces using a multitude of your own ideas!

History of beads

Archaeologists will tell you that beads and small pieces of pottery are supremely valuable to them as clues to the way people lived. Indeed, it is understood that man has drilled holes in stones and shells to use for adornment for more than 30,000 years.

Beads have always been a highly prized and widely-traded commodity. Moving from the Far East into the Middle East and Africa, from Europe into the New World, beads were traded for salt, spices, gold, and slaves: all the valued goods of different eras.

Bead loom, polyester thread, and "big eye" needle.

Tools, clockwise from top right: crimping pliers; split ring pliers; wire cutters; round nose pliers with side cutter; round nose pliers; flat nose pliers.

Individual beads have made extraordinary journeys over several centuries—take, for example, Venetian millefiore glass beads, which were made mainly during the eighteenth and nineteenth centuries. Many of these beads were taken to West Africa, often via Britain. From there they have been taken by traders to all parts of Africa and beyond. During the last century, many were taken back to African countries such as Nigeria and the Gambia where traders are currently operating businesses that send hundreds of tons of beads to America. Here they are sold at international bead shows where there are buyers from all over the world—including, no doubt, Italy!

Beads have been worn for protection; to show

status; as a way to carry wealth; and to send messages. Just as an Ashanti king wore his Chevron beads, or a Victorian widow wore jet beads, a teenage boy today with wooden beads round his neck is making a statement about himself.

Beautiful Beading contains step-by-step instructions for making beads. It also contains designs for bead jewelry using some of the wealth of beads that are currently being made all over the world. And it gives ideas for accessories that are decorated with beautiful beads.

Getting started

First you will need beads. You can make some, inspired by the ideas here, or you can buy them. There are now good bead shops and mail order catalogs all over the world. All the projects in this book are designed to be adapted to the beads that you find. The ideas in the accessories section are to inspire you to find your own objects to decorate.

You can work anywhere that has good light. Remember to protect yourself and others when you are cutting wire or metal, and to be careful not to inhale fumes from glues, paints, and polymer clays.

The tools, findings, and threads that are used in this book are set out for you. All of them are available from good bead shops or catalogs.

We have given you amounts for the projects shown in *Beautiful Beading*, but remember always to have extra supplies to hand: you may want to make a necklace longer, you may break a bead or damage a wire—it is better to be well prepared.

And the most important thing is to enjoy yourself!

Findings, from left to right beginning with the top row: sieve ear clips; eyepins; earwires; earscrews; earstuds; stud with hook and butterfly; necklace clasps; spring ends; french crimps; cufflink findings; split rings; barrette finding.

Making your own beads is great fun. The materials and techniques used here are intended to whet your appetite and fire your imagination. If you don't wish to start from scratch, however, you can buy beads and personalize them with some additional decoration.

MAKING BEADS

polymer clay

Polymer clay is probably the most popular material for making beads. It is sold under many different brand names: Fimo, Sculpey, and Cernit are a few of the brands that you may see on sale. It is an excellent material, as it can be used in very simple or very complex ways. In the following pages we demonstrate rolling and cutting, shaping and collaging, and using a mold.

1 Before using clay you need to condition it. Do this by cutting the clay into manageable sizes: quarter blocks are ideal. Then use your fingers and thumbs to work the clay from side to side until it begins to feel malleable. Roll it in a ball once it starts to feel reasonably soft.

Materials

4 x ¼ blocks of polymer clay
  (Fimo in this case)

Equipment

sharp blade
board or tile to work on
small roller
cocktail stick
foil tray covered in baking
  parchment

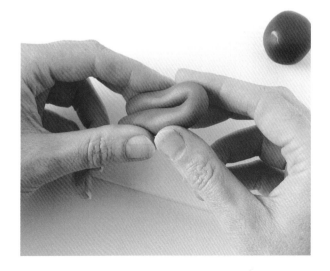

2 Roll a long "snake" out of your clay and then fold it back on itself. If the clay is correctly conditioned it will be pliable and there won't be any cracking or crumbling. Be careful as some clays are very soft and it is important not to overcondition them and make them mushy.

3 Make small flat rectangles out of the first two pieces that you have conditioned. When they are the same size place one piece on top of the other.

4 Cut these two pieces in half and stack them on top of each other again with the colors alternating.

5 Now use your fingers to roll up the layers of clay, remembering to decide which color you want on the outside.

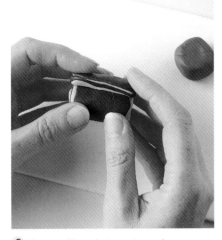

7 Now use the base of your palm to roll out the clay into a longer "snake." Stop when you have a good thickness for your beads, which will be made from slices of this roll (usually referred to as a cane). Now cut slices off the cane with your blade. Let the cane roll as you cut it so that you get neat slices. Keep half of this cane to make the striped spiral beads. Also, keep the ends where the spirals are uneven—all these scrap pieces will be used.

6 Keep rolling, but try to make sure that you can bring the outside layer right around the other layers. You may need to trim the inside layers a little. You will end up with a nice fat roll of striped clay.

8 Use a cocktail stick or a big needle to pierce the beads, pushing in from one side of the bead and then back into the hole from the other side. Place the beads on a foil tray that has been covered in baking parchment, making sure that they don't touch each other.

9 Now make the striped spiral bead. Condition the remaining two blocks of clay, and make a small stack of the four slices as you did before. Now cut slices off this block with your blade and wrap them around the remaining half of your cane. The slices should just touch each other around the cane.

10 This cane can now be rolled out to the diameter that you want for your beads. Again, keep half of this cane.

11 Squeeze these beads into squares, then pierce them. Roll the other half of the cane so that it is long and thin.

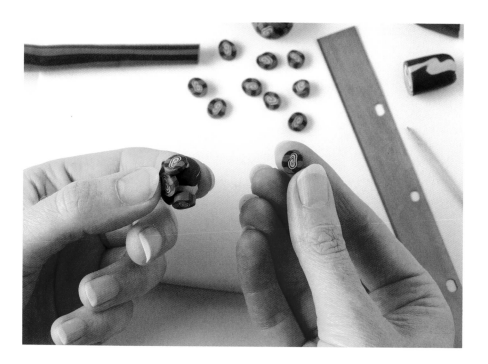

12 For the millefiore beads, cut the last section of cane into lots of very thin slices. Now make some of the scraps of clay into small balls. Cover these balls with the small slices of clay and use a finger to roll them against your palm to remove the lines, then pierce them with a cocktail stick. The beads can be baked in a domestic oven at a maximum temperature of 250°F. They need at least 20 minutes, but more time will make them stronger. It is important to follow the instructions on the packaging of your clay. Never bake at a higher temperature, and always have the room well ventilated. Remember to wash your hands after working with the clay.

shaping and collaging

Polymer clay can be shaped by hand into truly original figures.

1 There are many ways to use polymer clays. For example, the abstract bird used in the Bird and Beads Necklace on page 42 was shaped by hand then pierced and baked just like the beads on page 19. Just make the shape, pierce it and bake it as you have with the other polymer clay beads.

2 The plain beads in this choker were formed by hand and then textured by pressing sticks against them, and by pricking them. You can also collage items onto the clay beads before you bake them. On this piece the front of an old needle packet was pressed into the clay before baking. It was varnished after baking.

beads

These elegant cufflinks
were made using the
method shown on
pages 16–19.

using a mold

Another really exciting way to use polymer clays is to make molds from them. This method also makes use of your scraps of old clay.

1 Choose an item to use as a mold—simple shapes work best— and brush it with oil.

Materials

item of your choice for the shape
  (we have used an old buckle)
cooking oil
scraps of leftover polymer clay
1 x ½ block of silver Premo
good glue
stud earring findings
cufflink findings

Equipment

board or tile to work on
paint brush
foil tray covered in baking parchment
sharp blade
curved blade knife
round nose pliers

2 Now press a conditioned block of clay scraps over the item. This will need to be baked and allowed to cool before you finish your piece. The mold can then be used as many times as you like.

3 Brush the prepared mold with more oil, then press the conditioned silver clay into it. Make sure that you get the clay right into the mold.

4 Use the tip of your knife to help you get the clay back out of the mold. Now you can use your knife to trim around the shape that you have created. Repeat steps 3 and 4 to make a second piece for the cufflinks, then bake both pieces.

5 To make the molded shapes into cufflinks, glue a stud earring finding on to the back of each molded piece. When they are dry and secure gently roll the straight piece of the studs over, using the round nose pliers. Now you can open these loops sideways and attach cufflink findings.

air dry clay

Air dry clay can be bought
in blocks from craft shops. It
can be shaped and textured
and when it is dry you can paint
it or decorate it with varnishes
and powders.

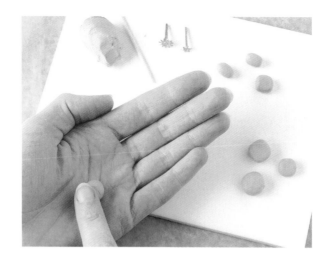

1 Pinch small pieces
of the clay and roll
them in your palm to
make round and oval
bead shapes.

2 Pierce them with
a stick to make the
holes then stamp
them. It is easier to
do this while the bead
is on the stick, as the
clay is quite soft.
Remove from the stick
and leave to dry.

Materials

a small amount from a block of air
   dry clay
gold and bronze powders
varnish

Equipment

cocktail stick
tiny stamps
sandpaper
paint brush

3 When the beads are dry, which
takes twelve hours or longer,
depending on size, sandpaper the
edges of the holes to make them
smooth. Dab small amounts of
metallic powder over the beads
then varnish them.

wire

You can make your own beads, pendant pieces, and spacer beads from lengths of wire. There is a huge assortment available from bead and hobby shops, so experiment with the different gauges and finishes.

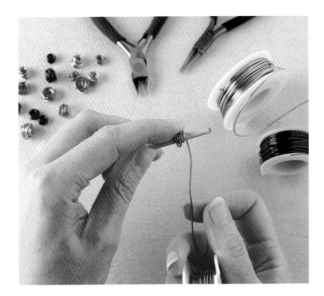

1 To make simple, wound wire beads wind the wire over your chopstick (or pencil) and also over itself. The aim is to get it closely looped and quite lumpy.

2 Take the bead off the chopstick and clip the wire off the roll. Now use your pliers to tuck the ends of the wire into the bead. Repeat steps 1 and 2 with the other wire.

Materials

18 gauge wire in two colors

Equipment

chopstick or pencil
wire cutters
round nose pliers

"gizmo" beads

These beads are made with a
clever and inexpensive tool called
a "gizmo" (patent pending) that
has been designed to take a lot
of the effort out of wire winding.

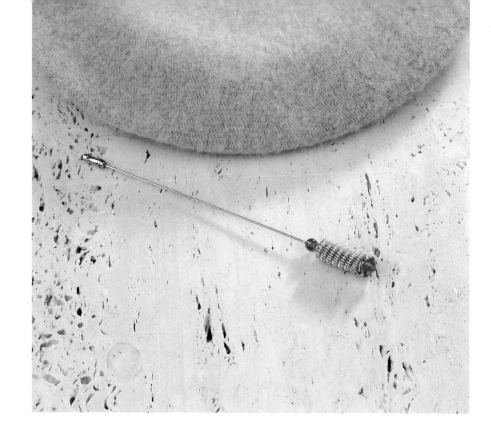

1 Attach the finer
wire to the smaller rod
on your gizmo and
wind it smoothly and
neatly along toward
the end. (You may find
it easier to clamp your
"gizmo" to the table.)

Materials

1 roll x 0.4 wire
1 roll x 0.8 wire

Equipment

"gizmo"
pliers
wire cutters

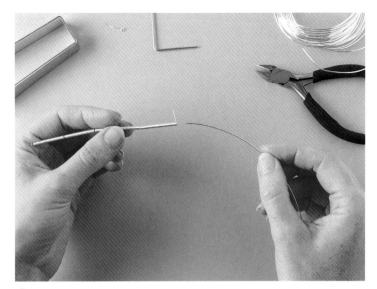

2 When you have a good length, take the coil off the rod and clip the ends. Cut about 1 ft. (30cm) of the thicker 0.8 wire and thread this into your coiled length.

3 Now attach this to the thicker rod on your "gizmo," and wind this until you have finished the coiled length. Wind on a little further with the thicker wire.

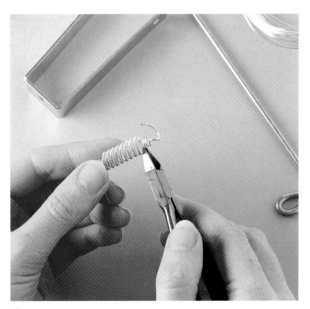

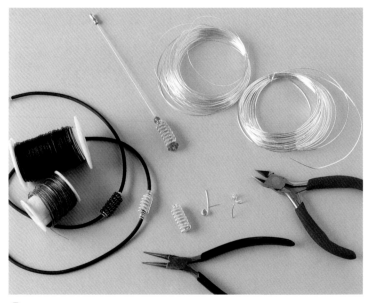

4 Use the wire cutters to tidy up the ends, and the pliers to tuck the ends into the beads.

5 The beads can be made in many different types of wire, and can be used in numerous ways, such as on chokers and hatpins.

copper sheet

Always wear thick gloves when
working with metal to protect your
hands from the sharp edges. You can
use all kinds of thin metal sheet, such
as soft drink cans, to make your beads.

Materials

A sheet of copper from a hobby shop

Equipment

ruler and felt pen
shears or very strong scissors
gloves
round nose pliers
hammer and block
chopstick

1 Start by marking up your bead
shapes on one side of the copper.
We have marked triangles that are about
2 in. (5.5cm) by 4¾ in. (12cm). Then cut
out the shape with your shears.

2 Use your pliers to fold in the edges of the shapes.

3 Now hammer the edges down: a smooth block will help you if you want the metal to be smooth, but you could try hammering on other surfaces to get different textures.

4 When the edges are smooth wind the triangle, from the broad end, around the chopstick.

5 You can either wind all the way to the end to make a smooth tubular bead, or you can use the round nose pliers to fold the pointed end in to create a more interesting shape.

6 The metal shapes can either be threaded through, or you can wrap wire around them to use them as pendant pieces.

wooden doweling

Lengths of doweling can be bought very cheaply from hardware stores. Doweling can be sawn into short lengths and then drilled down the middle. Once you have sanded down the ends, the beads can be colored and then threaded into a necklace. Try permanent marker pens, watered-down emulsion paints or spray paints. You can also experiment by gluing string or tiny beads to the pieces.

paper

Another cheap and easy way
to make your own beads is
to recycle all kinds of paper.

1 Start by marking up the bead
shapes on the back of the paper.
We have used triangles that are
8 in. x ¾ in.(20cm x 2cm). You can
alternate the shapes to make best
use of the paper.

2 When you have cut
out your triangles,
place glue on the back
of them, leaving about
0.2 in. (5mm) without
glue at the wide end.
Now roll the paper
triangles around your
cocktail stick. You
might need a little bit
more glue for the final
point. You can
strengthen the beads
by varnishing them.

Materials

wrapping paper
glue
varnish (optional)

Equipment

ruler and pencil
scissors
glue
cocktail stick

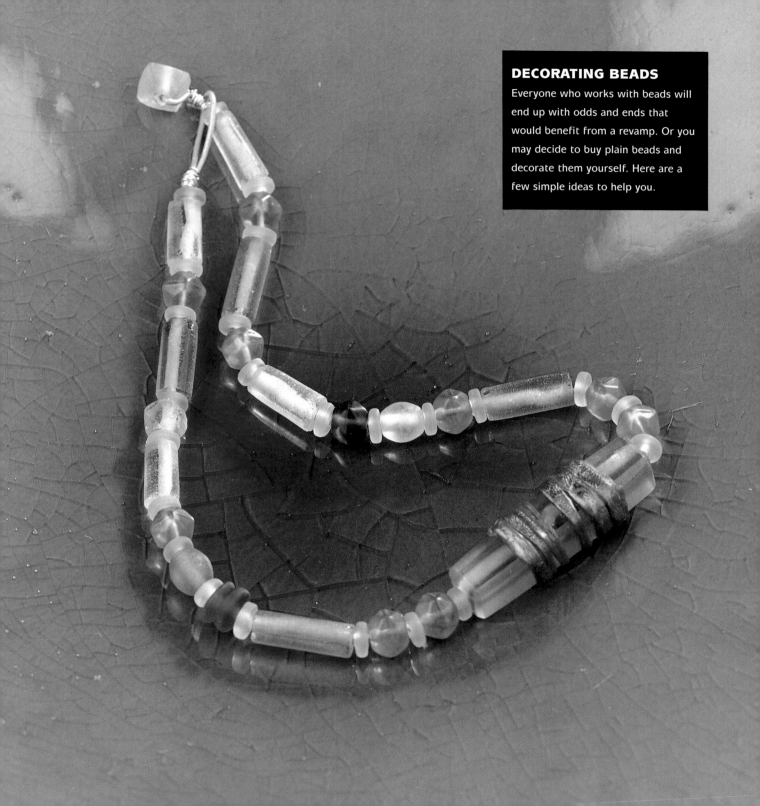

DECORATING BEADS

Everyone who works with beads will end up with odds and ends that would benefit from a revamp. Or you may decide to buy plain beads and decorate them yourself. Here are a few simple ideas to help you.

friendly plastic

These strips of heat-sensitive plastic come in a stunning range of colors and melt at quite low temperatures, making them easy and safe to use. Remember not to leave your decorated beads in a very hot place in case the plastic melts.

Materials

strips of friendly plastic (from a hobby shop)
plain beads

Equipment

2 dishes
small saucepan
scissors
chopstick

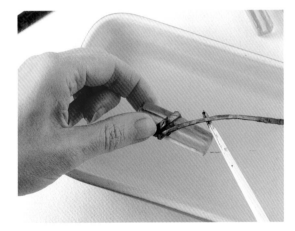

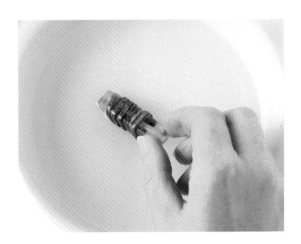

1 First get the plain beads and a dish of cold water ready, and heat some water in the saucepan. Then cut thin strips of friendly plastic, about 0.2 in. (5mm) wide. Make sure that you have plenty of strips as you will probably need to experiment a little with the water temperature to get the right amount of melting.

2 Pour hot (but not boiling) water into the other dish. Place the first strip of friendly plastic carefully into the hot water then, after a minute or so, gently lift one end of the strip out of the water with the chopstick. If it is beginning to melt, quickly wind the friendly plastic around the bead.

3 When it is all wound around the bead, press in the ends and drop the bead into the cold water to fix the friendly plastic.

papier mâché

You can use children's modeling material to make a "body" for these beads or you can decorate plain wooden beads as we have done here.

Materials

newspaper
wallpaper paste
plain round wooden beads
spray paint
permanent marker

Equipment

paint brush
cocktail stick
pot for the glue

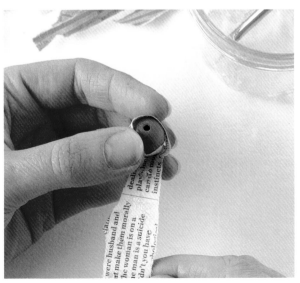

1 Tear some newspaper into strips and mix your paste. Brush lots of paste onto the newspaper and wrap layer after layer around the bead.

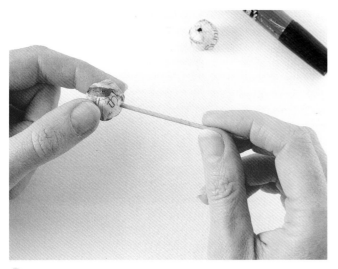

2 Use the cocktail stick to find the hole in your bead and pierce it before the paper dries. Repeat steps 1 and 2 until all the beads have been covered.

3 When the beads are dry you can paint them and decorate them as you choose.

string

Here is another simple idea for decoration. Place a strip of glue around the middle of some plain beads and wind string around them. When the glue is dry you can color the beads with paint or even nail varnish.

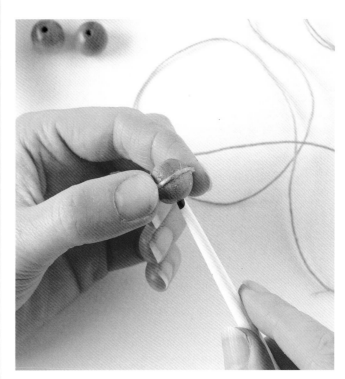

Materials

plain round wooden beads
glue
string

Equipment

chopstick
paint brush

making jewelry

the projects exactly, or apply some of the
techniques to your own particular designs.
Whichever way you choose to work, you will
create some truly stunning jewelry.

bird and beads necklace and earrings

This is an example of basic stringing and simple earring making. The necklace uses some of the polymer clay beads that were shown in the bead making section.

Materials

for the necklace

an assortment of beads made from
  polymer clay, horn, silver, and
  wood
a few small gray glass beads
25½ in. (65cm) x 0.024 "soft flex"
  thread
2 silver plate french crimps
silver or silver plate fastener

for the earrings

2 x 2 in. (5cm) silver plate eyepins
2 sterling silver earwires
an assortment of beads used in the
  necklace

Equipment

crimping pliers (or flat nose pliers)
round nose pliers
wire cutters

necklace

1 Thread your beads onto the "soft flex" thread. Start from the middle of the necklace and work up the sides. Hold the beads up against you and check in a mirror to see how the necklace will hang. Use tiny glass beads to break up the clusters of larger beads.

2 Leave about 1 in. (2.5cm) of thread at each end so that you can place the fastener on with french crimps. To do this place a crimp (or two if you are using smaller crimps) onto the thread at the end of the beads, guide the thread through the fastener and bring it back through the crimp. Squeeze this firmly with the crimping pliers.

3 Clip off the ends of the thread with your wire cutters. Check that you haven't left any gaps in your work and repeat the action on the other side of the necklace with the other piece of the fastener.

earrings

1 Place the beads that you have chosen for your earrings onto the eyepins, leaving about ¼ in. (8mm) of wire above the beads. Place the round nose pliers across the wire, against the top of the beads. Bend the wire toward you to an angle of about 45 degrees. Move your pliers up the wire and, using the tip of them, roll the end of the wire away from you to make a small loop in the wire. If you don't succeed in one movement you can take the pliers off the wire and make the movement again to finish your loop.

2 Open the loop on the earwire, sideways, with your pliers. Drop the earring piece into it and close the earwire up again. Repeat steps 1 and 2 for your other earring.

braided necklace and earrings

In this project three strands of beads are combined to create a dramatic, chunky necklace. On the following pages we also show you how to make matching earrings for a really exotic look.

necklace

Materials

for the necklace

pink "miracle" beads in three different sizes
pale pink coated beads
orange magatama beads (allow 3½ oz (100g))
small number of orange and red 8/0 rocailles
9 french crimps
fastener
4 silver plate tube beads for the ends
71 in. (180cm) x 0.014 "soft flex" thread

for the earrings

31½ in. (80cm) beading thread
4 french crimps
2 sieve earclips
a selection of beads used in the necklace

Equipment

wire cutters or scissors
crimping or flat nose pliers
masking tape

1 Cut the thread into three equal lengths and crimp them together about 2 in. (5cm) from one end. Start to thread on your beads in a random assortment of small clusters. Use more of the bigger beads as you get closer to the center of the threads. Keep two pink beads for the ends.

The large brooch is made in the same way as the earrings, but the barrette is made using strands of beads on fine wire, which are wound around the finding.

2 Place a crimp on each strand approximately 2 in. (5cm) from the end. Make sure that the crimps hold the beads neatly together.

3 Using a piece of masking tape to fix one end onto your worktop, braid all the strands together so that they fit neatly without gaps. Then crimp the three strands together.

4 Add the little silver plate tube and thread all of the strands through another pink bead. Crimp again and then cut off two of the threads.

earrings

5 Thread the second silver tube over these ends, and place another crimp over the last strand. Work the thread through the fastener and back through the crimp and squeeze the crimp firmly with your pliers. Now repeat the process at the other end of your necklace.

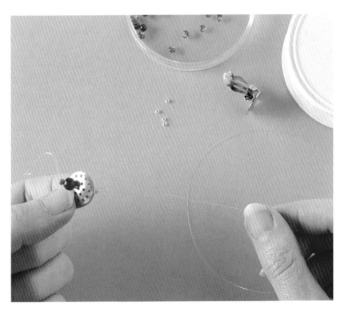

1 Cut 15¾ in. (40cm) of the beading thread and squeeze one of the crimps onto the end with your pliers. Thread from the back of your sieve, up through a larger central bead, and through a rocaille bead. Thread back through the central bead, but not the rocaille. This will keep the main bead in place.

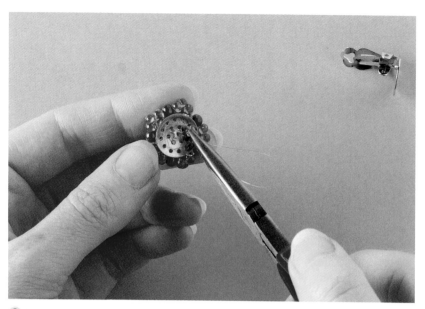

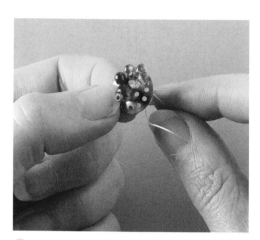

2 Add little clusters of other beads, threading in and out of the sieve and working around the central bead.

3 When you have filled all of the sieve, bring your thread through to the back and gently squeeze another crimp onto the end, making sure that all the beads on the front are firmly in place.

4 Place the back of the earring in position, then use your pliers to fold the little flaps on the sieve over the earring back to hold it in place. Repeat steps 1 to 4 to make the second earring.

knots necklace

This necklace is designed to show how a few beads can make a great impact when combined with a sympathetic thread.

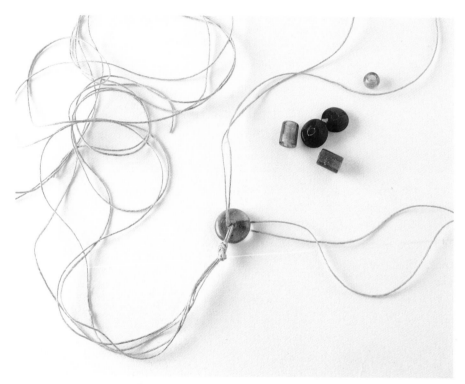

1 Cut four 2¼ yard (2 meter) lengths of the hemp, and thread them through the central bead, so that you have four strands at each side. Make a knot on either side of the bead.

Materials

17 assorted glass beads with largish
  holes
9⅓ yards (8.25 meters) hemp
  thread

Equipment

scissors
thick needle
masking tape

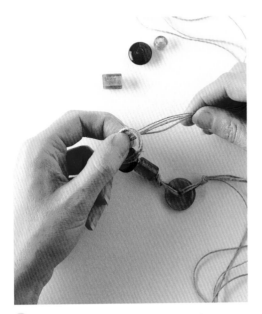

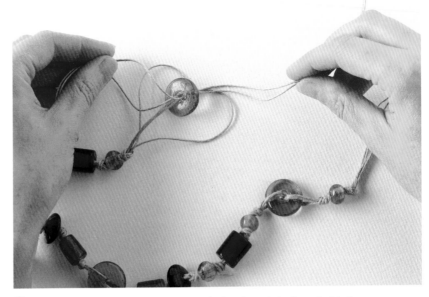

2 Add beads to each side, knotting between each one as you work. You are using a simple overhand knot, made over your finger (see diagram on page 122). You can insert a needle into the knots and guide them into place beside the beads if you wish.

3 To thread the other ring beads, work the threads in from behind and in front of the central bead and cross them in the middle.

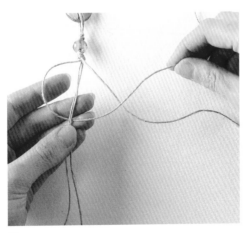

4 Tape the necklace to the worktop, and make half knots for the ends (see diagram on page 122). These will form an attractive spiral.

5 Lay down the two shortest threads as the core threads, and work with the other two. Work them left under the core and over the right; right over the core and back under the left.

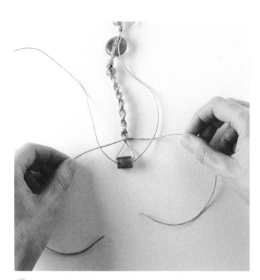

6 About 1¼ in. (3cm) from your final length stop knotting and add in a fastener bead by using the core threads. The core threads should now be folded back on themselves to face the center of the necklace. Complete the knotting, on this side, on top of them.

7 On the other side stop knotting at the same point as before, leave a gap and then use your final section of thread to make a small length of buttonhole stitch over the core threads (see diagram on page 122). Knot down over these threads as before.

8 Your ends will look like this. Use your needle or a small piece of bent wire to work the loose ends back into the knotting, then trim them.

clay beads necklace

This design uses the air dry clay beads that were shown in the first section of the book (see page 25). Again, the threads are an important feature of the necklace, so a few beads go a long way.

Materials

5½ yards (5 meters) gray thread
a selection of different clay beads (about twenty)
small brown square beads (twice as many as clay beads)
8/0 gold rocailles (twice as many again)

Equipment

thick needle

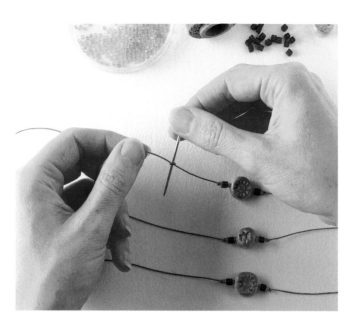

1 Cut 3 x 35½ in. (90cm) lengths of the thread, and lay them out on your worktop. Thread your central beads onto the threads, place the little beads either side, then make a knot beside them. As in the Knots Necklace project, you are making overhand knots. Now leave spaces before your next knots. To position the knots insert a needle into them and gently draw them into place.

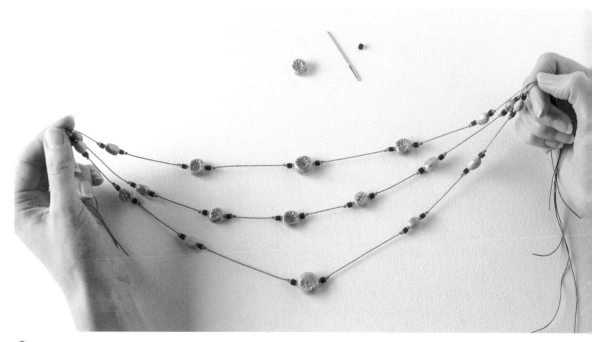

2 When you have got all your beads knotted onto the necklace hold the strands up to see what lengths you need them to be before you start to make your knotted ends.

3 Cut another 31½ in. (80cm) of thread and lay the middle of it behind your strands. Knot all these strands together, positioning the knot with a needle if necessary. Then start to work your knotting. This time you are making square knots (see diagram on page 122), which will lie flat.

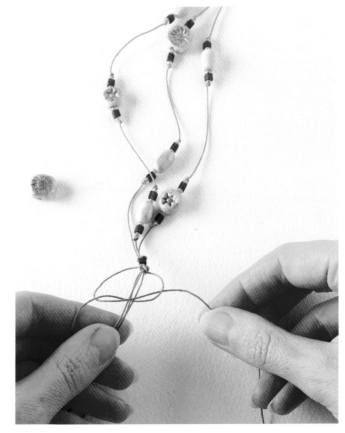

4 Now work with the two ends of the new thread that you have added, with your three original strands as the core. Work left under the core and over the right thread, right over the core and back under the left. Then reverse this: left over the core and under the right, right under the core and over the left.

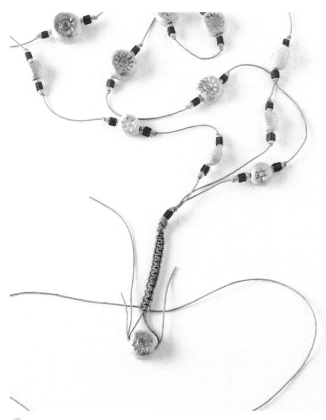

6 Keep knotting at the other end of the necklace, turn the end back on itself to create a loop, and then knot back on top of your band to secure it.

5 Place two core threads through one side of the fastener bead, one through the other. Bring them around toward the middle of the necklace and knot them in, just as you did with the Knots Necklace (see step 6 on page 53).

7 Finish off all of the loose ends by sewing them back into the band with your needle and then trimming them. Your necklace ends will look like this.

copper pendant

We took two of the copper sheet beads from the first section of the book (see page 30) and combined them with some gunmetal wire to create an elegant pendant. This was then threaded onto jewelry cable, which complements the copper and gunmetal of the pendant.

1 Cut about 20 in. (50cm) of the 22 gauge wire. Leaving a 2 in. (5cm) "tail," wrap the wire a few times around the two copper sheet beads .

Materials

22 gauge gunmetal wire
2 copper sheet beads
2.5mm silver plate beads
jewelry cable (to the length that you require)
2 leather crimps
2 split rings
fastener

Equipment

round nose pliers
flat nose pliers
wire cutters
split ring pliers (optional)

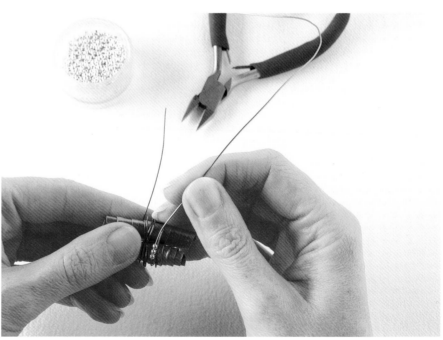

2 Start to thread a few of the tiny silver beads onto the wire as you wrap it around the front of the copper beads.

3 When you have securely wrapped the beads so that they sit well together, wind the end of the wrapping wire around the straight piece of wire at the top of the beads. Snip off the excess, then thread another silver bead onto the straight piece.

4 Place the round nose pliers above the bead, to create a gap, then bend the wire toward you.

5 Make a loop of wire around the pliers, then wrap the end of the wire back against the silver bead. Flatten the edges under the loop with the flat nose pliers. To angle the wire around the beads, place the tips of the pliers either side of the wire and twist them 45 degrees. This is decorative and also tightens the wire.

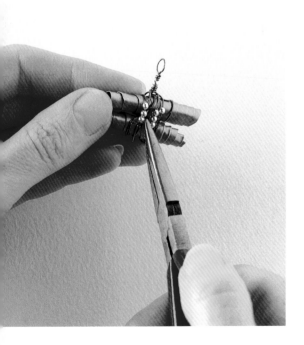

6 Cut a length of the jewelry cable to suit you, and attach a leather crimp to it with the flat nose pliers.

7 Now unravel the cable into its seven separate strands with your fingers.

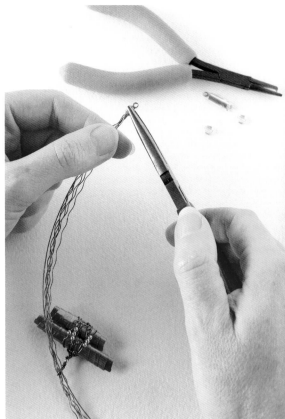

8 Thread on the pendant piece that you have made and place a leather crimp onto the other end of the cable.

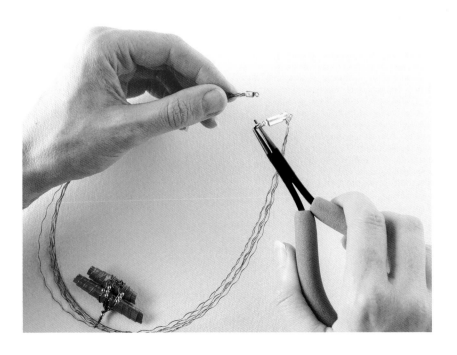

9 Use the split ring pliers to attach the split rings and the fastener to the cable. You can do this without the pliers, which are specially designed to prise the split rings apart, but your fingernails are likely to suffer!

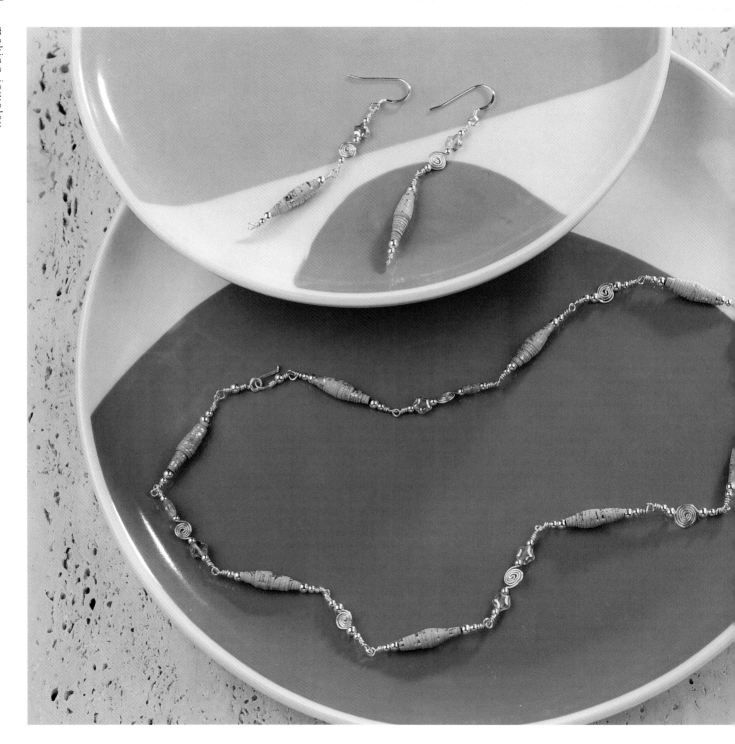

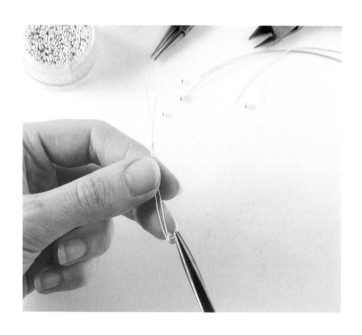

paper bead chain

This project also uses beads made in the first section of the book (see page 34). It is a delicate chain of wire, paper beads, and silver beads. Although this is quite a complicated necklace to make, you will learn a lot about wire.

1 We cut 7 x 6 in. (15cm), 8 x 4 in. (10cm), and 2 x 4¾ in. (12cm) lengths of wire to make the necklace that is shown. Remember that you might like to make it longer or shorter and may not need the full length of the pieces of wire, but always be generous with the length of each piece. Start with one of the 6 in. (15cm) pieces, fold it over on itself, not quite in half, and start to make a coil in the center. Do this by making a neat curl with the round nose pliers, then holding this with the flat nose pliers. Use your fingers to curl the two strands of wire around the center to build up the coil.

2 When you have made a neat coil, bend the ends of the wire out at either side of it. Now thread two silver beads onto one side and make a closed link in the end of the wire. To do this make a loop a little way from the beads and then wrap the end of the wire down toward them. Clip the last piece off and neaten the end with the flat nose pliers (see diagram on page 122).

Materials

11 yard (10 meter)
0.6 silver plate wire
2.5mm and 3mm silver
plate beads
paper beads
small glass stars

Equipment

wire cutters
round nose pliers
flat nose pliers

3 Repeat this on the other side of your first section, then add the next link. Take a 4 in. (10cm) length of wire and make a closed loop at the bottom—remembering to drop one end of the first section into the loop before you wrap it. Thread more silver beads and a paper bead above this, then make a closed loop at the other end of the wire.

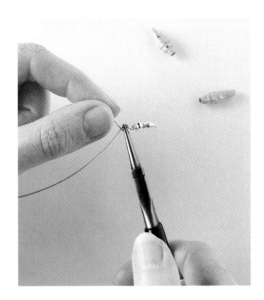

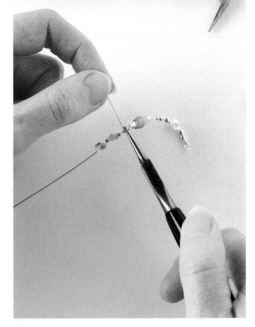

4 Now make another coil section, thread a small star in with the silver beads this time, and make a closed loop that links back into the previous section. Continue in this way on either side of the necklace, alternating the sections and linking them into each other.

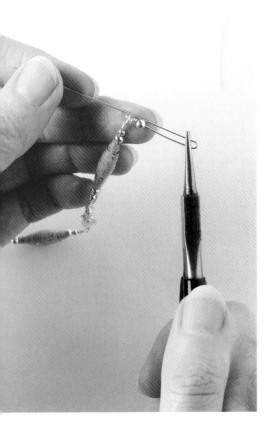

5 You can make your own fastener too. Use one of the 4¾ in. (12cm) pieces of wire and make a closed loop to link it to the end of your chain. Thread on a 3mm silver bead, then fold the rest of the wire back on itself 1 in. (2.5cm) from the bead.

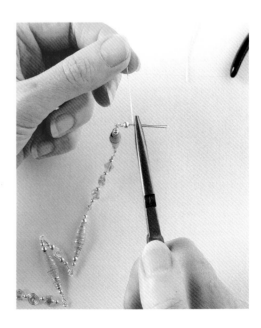

6 Place the flat nose pliers across both the wires very slightly above the bead and wrap the long end back down toward it.

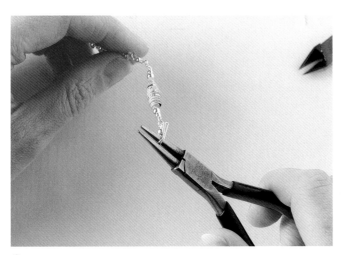

7 Bend this double length of wire around the round nose pliers to make a hook shape, and flick out the end of the hook to finish this side of the fastener.

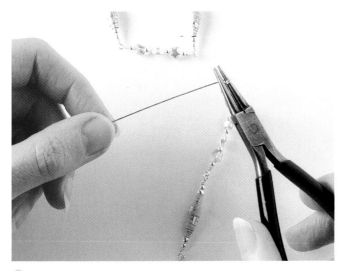

8 On the other side you need an "eye," so make the closed loop again, add a silver bead, then place your pliers against the wire to create a space above the bead. Now move your pliers up the wire and wrap the end twice around the nose of the pliers. Hold these two loops sideways with the flat nose pliers, gently so you don't spoil the shape, then wrap the end of the wire back down to the bead. Neaten this with the flat nose pliers.

Matching earrings can be made in the same way as the necklace—use two sections of the chain and add an earwire to the top.

wrapped stone pendant

This design will extend your skill with wire. We have chosen a simple stone triangle and wrapped it with wire, but you could find other alternatives—a semi-precious donut or a kiln glass circle bead would look good. Or make your own shape from polymer clay for a truly unique piece.

1 Take the piece of thinner wire and make a coil that is the size of the hole in the center of your piece. Now wrap the wire twice around one edge of the piece, going back through the coil in the center.

Materials

20 in. (50cm) x 0.6 wire
6¾ in. (17cm) x 0.8 wire
1 limestone triangle with hole
  in the center
1 small silver bead
2 large spring ends
rubber thong
fastener

Equipment

wire cutters
round nose pliers
flat nose pliers

2 Wrap the wire twice around another edge of the stone and once on the final edge.

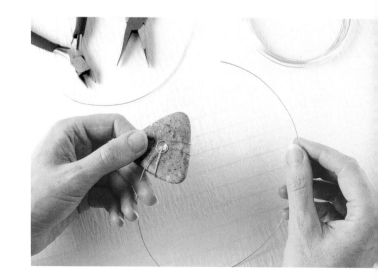

3 Now add the thicker length of wire. Fold it around the edge that you are working on and wrap one end around the straight end of wire above the stone piece.

4 Wrap the thinner wire around the other side of the thick wire, then wrap the end over the top of the thick wire above the stone piece.

5 Neaten these wraps of wire and thread on the silver bead. Roll the end of the thick wire around the widest part of the round nose pliers to form a loop big enough for the rubber thong to go through. Wrap the wire back down to the top of the bead.

6 Now angle all the wrapped wire with your flat nose pliers. Place the pliers across each strand in different places and turn them about 45 degrees. Take care not to scratch the stone piece or snap the wire.

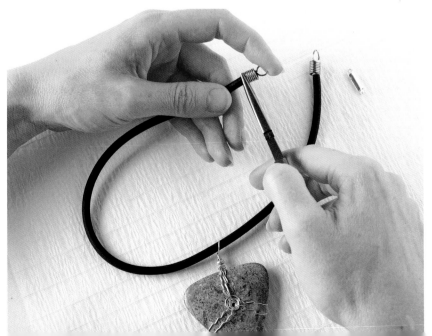

7 Fit the large spring ends over the length of rubber and squeeze in their final rings to attach them to it. Add the fastener by opening the loops on it sideways and slot them onto the spring ends of the rubber thong.

amethyst earrings and bracelet

A good contrast—delicate earrings and a really powerful bracelet with matching stones. The necklace in the photograph opposite is made by threading oval amethyst beads and ornate silver beads onto 0.014 "soft flex" thread, then crimping a silver plate fastener to the ends.

earrings

Materials

for the earrings

15¾ in. (40cm) x 0.6 silver plate wire
round and oval amethyst beads
small ornate silver beads
6¼ in. (16cm) x 0.6 or 0.8 sterling silver wire
2 butterfly backs to fit (optional)

for the bracelet

23½ in. (60cm) memory wire
2 triple spacer bars
6mm amethyst beads
oval amethyst beads
decorative silver beads
60 in. (150cm) x 0.4 silver plate wire
fastener

Equipment

strong wire cutters
pen
file (optional)
flat nose pliers
round nose pliers

1 Cut six lengths of the 0.6 silver plate wire wire about 2½ in. (6 or 7cm) long. Make a small coil at the bottom of each of the pieces and thread on the amethyst and decorative silver beads. Make groups of three with slightly different lengths within the groups, then make a closed loop at the top of each piece. (You can learn the techniques for the coils and the closed loops in the Paper Bead Chain on page 63.) Cut two 3 in. (8cm) lengths of the sterling silver wire to make earwires. Make a little loop about ¾ in. (2cm) from the end of each piece.

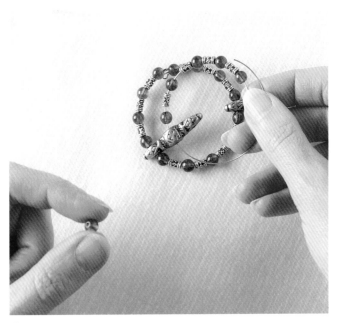

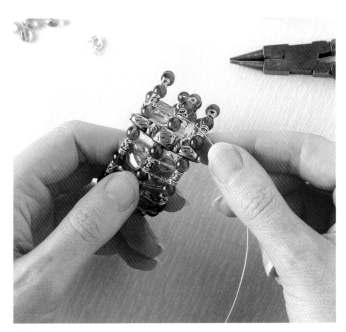

4 Now thread beads onto the next piece of memory wire and thread this into the next hole on the spacer bar. Your central wire should be the long one.

5 When you have all three rows of beads ready, cut three 20 in. (50cm) lengths of the 0.4 wire. Starting at one end, attach it to the top strand of memory wire so that it sits between the beads. Now wind it around each row of the bracelet, threading an oval amethyst bead between each row. Add the extra sections of the wire as you need them.

6 Press in the ends of the wire neatly so that your bracelet is smooth. Add the fastener to the longer central row.

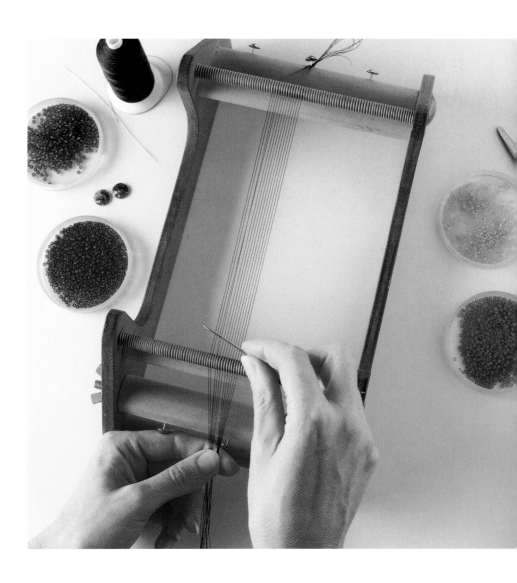

striped woven bracelet

To make this bracelet you will need a beadloom. The one in the photograph below is quite a sophisticated version, but simpler ones are available from beadstores and hobbyshops. Once you have learnt to use your loom, working out your own designs is easy.

1 Start by threading the loom. Cut 13 strands of thread, 23½ in. (60cm) long, and tie them together at one end. Separate the threads into the slots at each end of the loom so that they are opposite each other and there are no gaps between them. Tie the threads around the other end of the loom, then tighten the loom so that they are as taut as possible.

Materials

fine black polyester thread
4 colors of 8/0 matt rocailles (you
  will need 3½ oz (100g) bags of
  the main colors and ¾ oz (20g)
  bags of the others)
2 buttons

Equipment

scissors
beadloom
"big eye" needle
fine needle

2 Now thread a comfortable length of thread onto the "big eye" needle, and pick up twelve of the rocailles. Hold them under each of the spaces between the threads.

3 Draw the needle through the rocailles, remembering to leave a longish tail of thread, then work the needle back through from the other side. This time make sure that your needle and thread pass *over* the threads (see diagram on page 123).

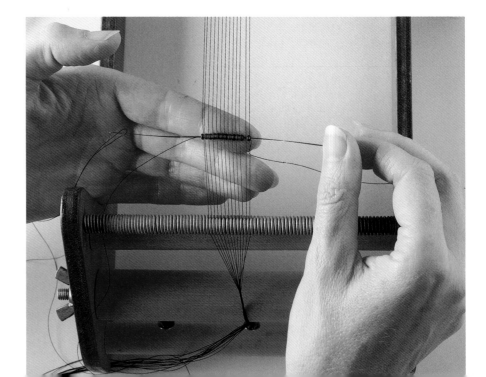

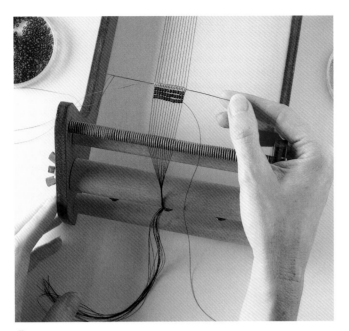

4 Repeat steps 2 and 3 for each row of beads. The first few will be difficult to keep in place, but the weaving soon becomes easy. Change colors as you work, and add in more thread as you need it. Always leave long tails on the new threads so that you can work them back in later.

5 When you have made the right length of bracelet for you, allowing for the fasteners, loosen the loom and take the band off.

6 Undo the knots at the ends of the band and thread two of the warp threads into the "big eye" needle. Thread a row of rocailles onto these, and work through one of the buttons. Now work back down the rocailles and secure the threads. Repeat the process at the other edge of the band.

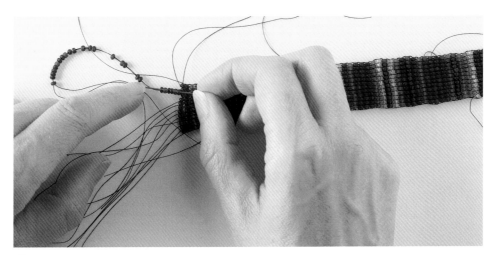

7 Thread your needle onto the threads at the other end to create two loops that are big enough to go around the buttons. Thread on the rocailles and work back into the strand when the loop is the right size. Again, secure these threads.

9 To make an edging for the band thread a rocaille onto the fine needle, pick up the outside warp thread between rows and thread back up into the rocaille. Continue in this way until you have made an edging all around the bracelet.

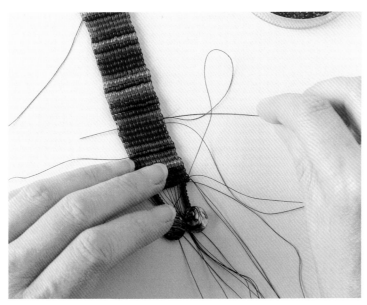

8 Now the boring bit—all of the loose threads need to be worked back into the band a few times before you can trim them.

aquamarine chip choker

This is a piece of jewelry that requires patience, but is well worth the effort. All of the weaving is done by hand, and the design is built up stage by stage, with very glamorous results.

Materials

polyester thread
3½ oz (100g) bag 5mm bugles
  (glass tubes)
¾ oz (20g) 8/0 rocailles
4 x 6mm moonstone beads
a string of aquamarine chips

Equipment

scissors
fine needle

1 Start by weaving the band. There are two of the little bugles (tubes) on each row, so thread four then thread back into the first two. Take your needle back down the next two so that you now have two rows side by side.

2 Add another two bugles to the thread and work into the second row again then back into the third. Continue in this way building the band until it is long enough for your neck, allowing for the fasteners.

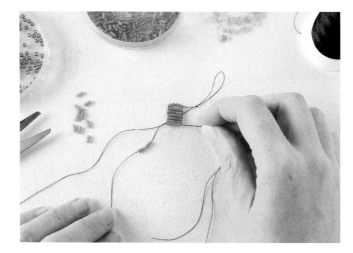

turquoise and silver multistrand necklace

This necklace is simple to make but creates a very dramatic cluster of turquoise and silver beads. The real turquoise beads range in shape from chips to chunks, and we have added turquoise ceramic beads so that the necklace won't cost a fortune to make.

Materials

about 10 ft. (3 meters) x 0.014
 "soft flex" thread
17 turquoise beads in assorted
 sizes
11 turquoise discs
6 x 4mm round turquoise beads
10 turquoise chips
46 turquoise ceramic tubes
32 small Balinese silver beads
6 x 3mm silver plate
 round beads
146 tiny silver plate french crimps
2 large silver plate french crimps
2 silver plate calottes
a length of silver chain
 (cut in two)
1 clasp

Equipment

wire cutters
crimping pliers or flat nose pliers

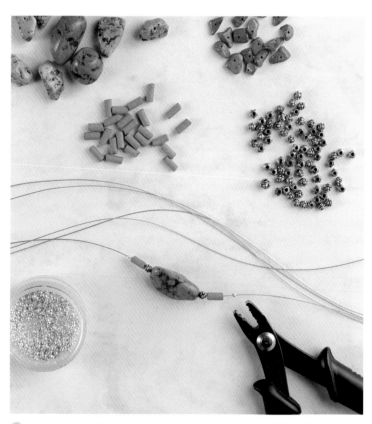

1 Cut the "soft flex" into five graduating lengths and lay them out on a work surface. Start by threading the largest bead onto the longest strand. Hold it in position by squeezing one of the small french crimps onto either side of the thread. You can do this with crimping pliers if you have them, or with flat nose pliers.

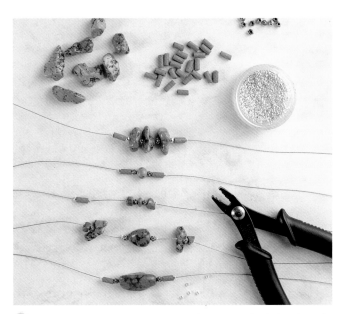

2 Work up the pattern of your beads onto each of the threads, leaving gaps between the clusters of beads and holding them in place with the small crimps.

3 Hold up the strands of beads as you work to see how the balance of your design is developing. It is also a good idea to hold them against you and look in a mirror to see the effect that you are creating.

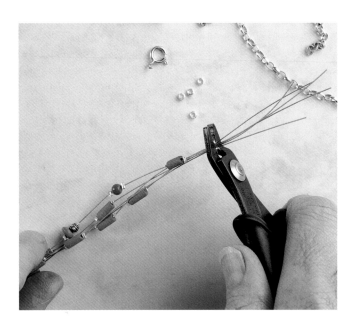

4 Once you are happy with the positioning of the strands, hold them together and firmly squeeze one of the large french crimps into place over all of the strands. Repeat this on the other side of your work, and trim off the loose ends.

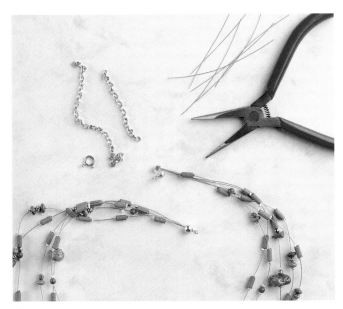

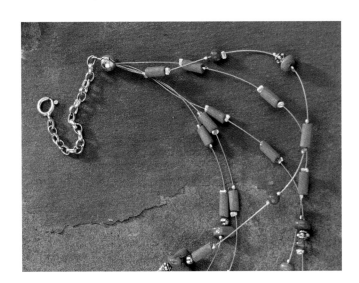

5 Position a calotte over each end and squeeze each one onto the threads with the crimp securely inside. Be careful not to be too forceful or you may damage the threads.

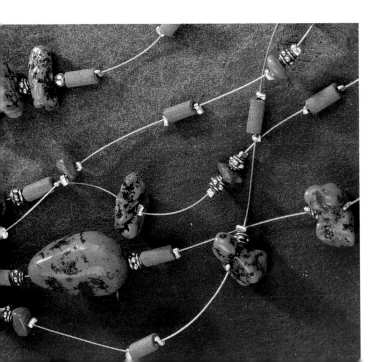

6 Open the loop on the top of the calotte and drop in the end of a piece of chain, then close the loop again. Repeat this for the other end and add a clasp to one side. The clasp can be fastened through different links in the chain to allow the necklace to be worn at different lengths.

decorating objects

that you can decorate: you may not find exactly the same items, but if you look around you should find some interesting objects to enhance, using the techniques described.

windchimes

These elegant windchimes are made from tubes of metal that are available from bead shops or hobbyshops. You could work on a larger scale using piping from a hardware store. Hung outdoors, the windchimes make a lovely noise and the delicate glass beads make them colorful too.

Materials

circular piece of wood sprayed
   silver, with 0.12 in. (3mm) holes
   drilled into it close to the edge,
   plus a hole in the center
metal tubes cut to different lengths
2¾ yards (2.5 meters) x 0.019
   "soft flex" thread
1 crystal drop
french crimps
small bag 6/0 rocailles
strong glass beads

Equipment

drill
metal saw for the tubes
clamp
safety glasses
file
crimping pliers
wire cutters

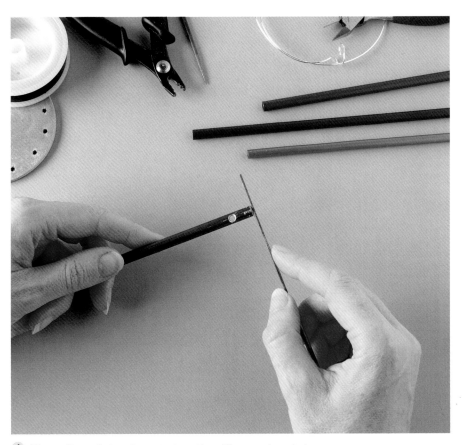

1 First collect all the elements together. The wooden circle should be colored and have the required holes drilled into it. The tubes should be sawn to different lengths, and have a hole drilled through one end. It is easier to do this if you clamp them first: remember to wear safety glasses when cutting the metal. File off any rough edges on the tubes.

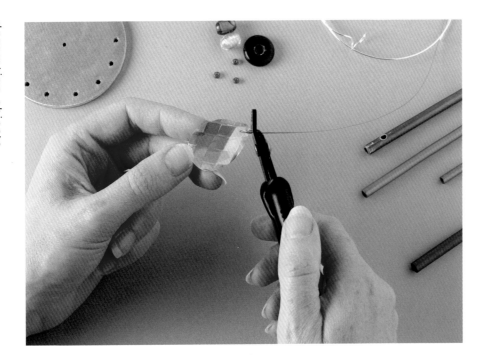

2 Now string the crystal to hang in the center. We have used a piece of the "soft flex" about 14 in. (35cm) long, but your proportions may be different. Use a crimp to secure the crystal and add a rocaille above the crimp.

3 Place another crimp onto the middle of this thread, then thread on a few more beads. Bring the end up through the center of the wooden circle, place on a rocaille and crimp securely above it so that the piece hangs from the disk. Make your other beaded pieces so that they can be hung in the same way, at different lengths.

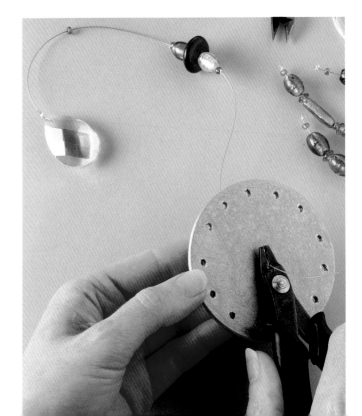

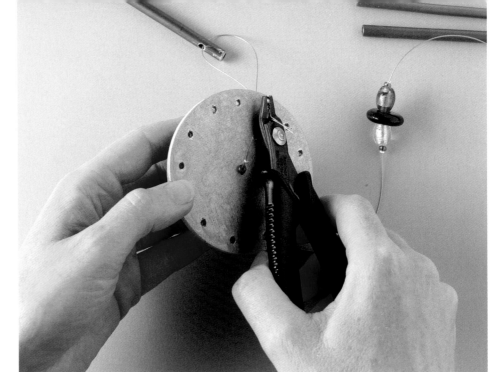

4 To attach the first tube to the disk, loop a length of thread through the hole you have made at the end of the tube. Thread a rocaille onto both strands to keep them together. Bring these ends through one of the holes in the circle, and crimp them to secure the tube.

5 When all your pieces are hanging together well, clip off the ends of the "soft flex."

To create two loops from which to hang the windchimes, take two short pieces of thread and crimp them back through the circle, from the top, at opposite sides.

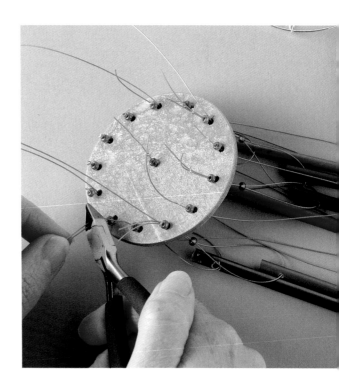

daisy candle holder

This candle holder was quite stark, but the beads have completely transformed it. We've made quite a bold design, but you could opt for more delicate beads to achieve a different look.

Materials

43 in. (110cm) x 18 gauge
  gunmetal jewelry wire
round and disk shaped glass beads
4 big glass daisies
a few blue rocailles

Equipment

wire cutters
flat nose pliers
round nose pliers

1 Cut two 21½ in. (55cm) lengths of the wire. Start by winding it around one of the bars, then flatten it against the bar with the flat nose pliers.

2 Thread on a few glass beads then wrap the wire around the round nose pliers to make a loop that will hold the beads in place.

3 The daisy comes next. Thread the wire through the center and through another glass bead, then back through the center of the daisy so that the central bead will hold the daisy in place.

4 Now make more little clusters of beads with loops beneath them, and take the wire around the corner of the candle holder.

5 Work back up the other side of the candle holder in the same way, heading for the far corner. Wind the end of this piece of wire around the top bar to finish it off. Repeat this on the other two sides with the other piece of wire.

6 As a final touch, sprinkle some rocailles onto the night light so that they will float in the wax as it melts.

kitsch frame

This is a simple idea for brightening up a very basic frame. The beads are stuck on to the frame so don't use valuable beads—something glitzy is what you need!

Materials

plain wooden frame
coated beads and stars in
  different colors
silver colored daisy beads

Equipment

2 felt pens
strong multi-purpose glue
a needle or cocktail stick

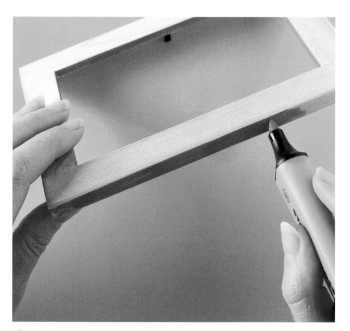

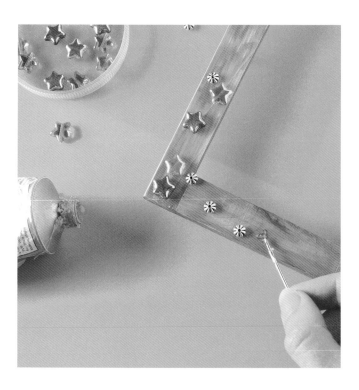

1 Start by coloring the frame with the felt pens.

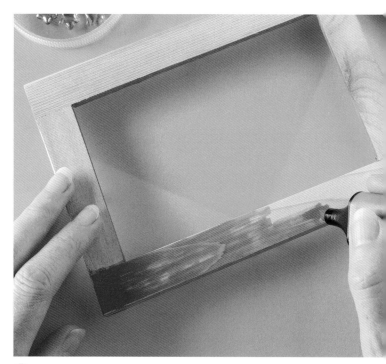

2 Remember to go inside and outside the frame using two contrasting colors.

3 Dab small dots of glue on the frame and maneuver the beads into place with your needle.

tiara frame

Making this more elaborate frame will also extend your wireworking skills. The wirework looks very grand on the frame, but remember that you could adapt it to fit on a hairband to make a tiara.

Materials

silver picture frame 7 in. (18cm) wide
17¾ in. (45cm) x 1.0 silver plate wire
8 in. (20cm) x 0.8 wire
2.5mm and 3mm silver plate beads
2¼ yards (2 meters) x 0.4 wire
a small assortment of coated beads
3 star beads
strong tape

Equipment

wire cutters
flat nose pliers
round nose pliers

1 Cut 17¾ in. (45cm) of 1.0 wire and bend it in half. Hold the wire still with the flat nose pliers about 1 in. (3cm) below the bend. With the round nose pliers in your other hand, twist the wire a few times leaving a small loop at the top.

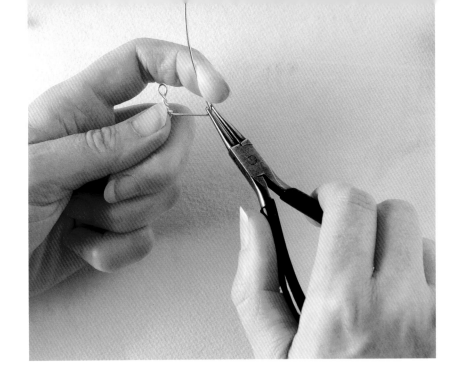

2 Make a right angle at the bottom of the twisted wire by holding the wire with the pliers and bending the end up with your fingers. Then make another right angle about 1 in. (3cm) further along the wire.

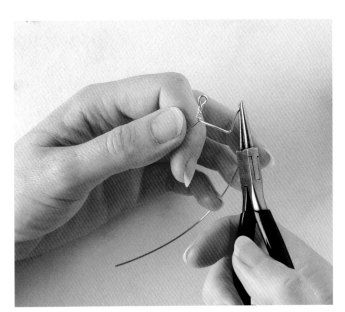

3 Fold the end of the wire around the round nose pliers and back down toward you.

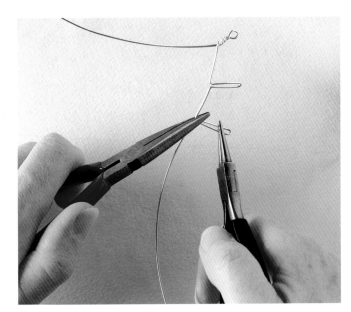

4 Move along the wire and twist the next fold using two pairs of pliers.

5 Make one more shorter fold and
repeat steps 2 to 4 on the other half of
the wire, so that the two sides match.
Measure the piece of wire against the
top of the frame and make one last
angle at each side of the wire so that
the tiara is just slightly narrower than
the top of the frame. Cut the 0.8 wire
and make a tiny spiral at one end of it.

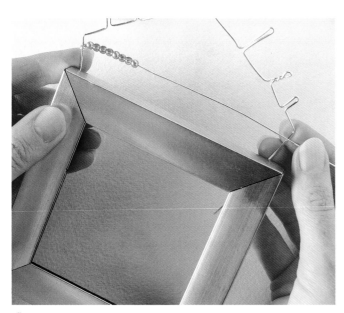

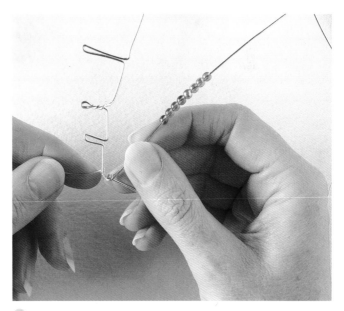

6 Thread some coated beads onto the short piece of wire,
then slide one end of the tiara through the spiral you made in
the last step. Hold the short piece of wire against the other side
of the tiara and make a second spiral where both wires meet.

7 Thread the other end of the tiara through the second spiral.
Cut 27½ in. (70cm) of 0.4 wire, wind it on to the corner of the
top wire, make it secure and then wrap it until you come to the
first fold.

8 Thread some of the silver beads and coated beads onto the wire and take it around the straight wire at the bottom. Add more beads, bring the wire back up to the top and wrap it along the tiara toward the next fold.

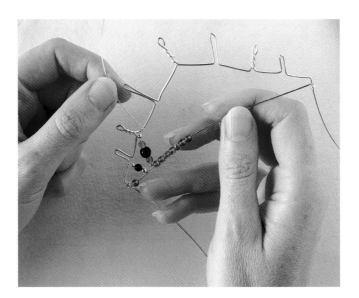

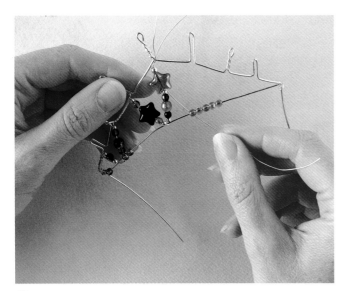

9 Continue in this way, remembering to separate out the beads on the bottom wire, until you have threaded a star and brought the wire up by the top spiral. Finish this wire off neatly around the top and cut another 27½ in. (70cm) piece of the 0.4 wire. Attach this to the wire at the other side of the spiral and thread it back down through the star bead. Work on toward the other side of the tiara.

10 Finish your piece by making a neat angle at each side of the wire so that the tiara will sit on top of the frame. Now tape it securely to the back of the frame.

napkin ring and decorated jug

Here are a few ideas for decorated tableware. The napkin rings are made in gourd stitch worked over a cord. The jug has a little elasticated "necklace" made for it. To complete the set, you could embroider some napkins with matching beads.

Materials

for the napkin ring

white cotton cord
white polyester thread
8/0 transparent rainbow rocailles
  (3½ oz (100g) will make several
  napkin rings)
oval coated bead (1 per napkin ring)

for the decorated jug

8/0 and 6/0 transparent rainbow
  rocailles
7 x 1.48 in. (38mm) eyepins
"stretch magic" thread
oval coated beads
one french crimp

Equipment

fine needle
scissors
round nose pliers
flat nose pliers

napkin ring

1 Cut a length of the cord long enough to go around the napkin, leaving space for the decorative bead in the center. Cut a length of the white polyester thread and make a knot in it leaving a loose tail. Thread on three of the rocailles and work a couple of rows in gourd stitch—to do this thread a fourth bead and work back into the first; thread a fifth and work back into the second; sixth into the third; seventh into the fourth bead, and so on (see diagram on page 123).

2 After a few rows increase the number of rocailles by threading on two beads before you thread into each bead on the row before.

3 You will have formed a little cone by now. Slip the cord into this cone and carry on beading around it.

4 From time to time, make a small stitch in the cord to secure the work.

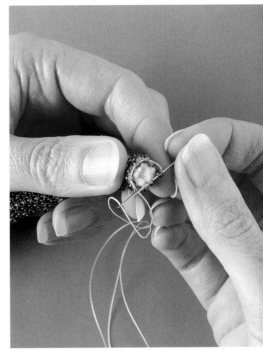

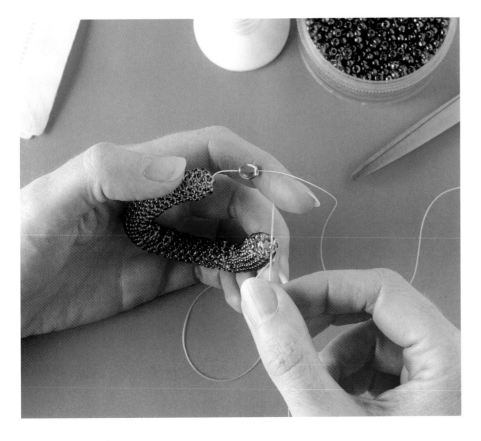

5 When you have covered the cord, reduce the rocailles back to three by threading into every other one for one row. Then do a couple more rows to cover the end of the cord.

6 Finally, sew into the oval bead and pass the thread through the end of the cord. Tighten to close the circle. Finish off with one or two stitches.

decorated jug

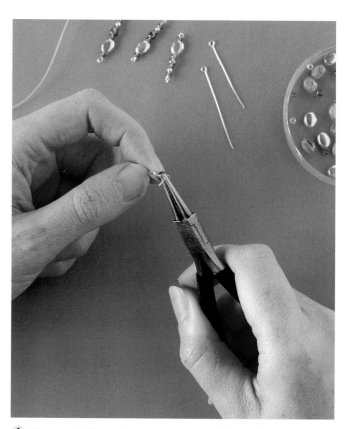

1 Thread a 6/0 rocaille onto an eyepin followed by a coated oval bead. Then add another 6/0 rocaille followed by an 8/0 rocaille and three 6/0 rocailles

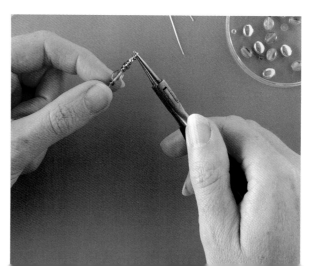

2 Roll the top of the wire with the round nose pliers to secure the beads and make a loop. Repeat for the other six eyepins.

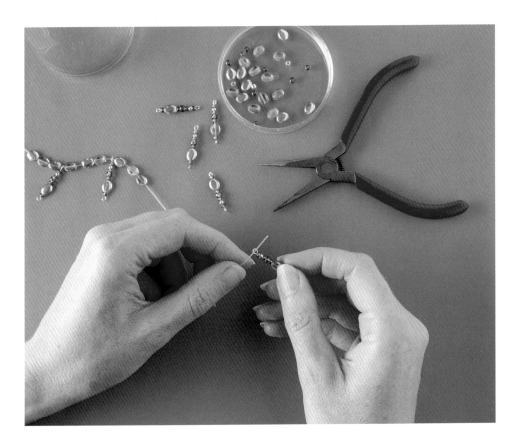

3 Cut a length of "stretch magic" to go comfortably around the jug without stretching too much. Allow ¾ in. (2cm) either side for finishing. Thread on enough of the oval beads to encircle the jug, adding the hanging pieces as you go.

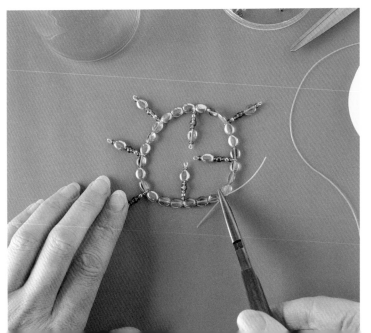

4 Place both ends of the thread through a crimp and squeeze it gently with your pliers so that you don't damage the elasticated thread. Cut off the loose ends and slide the decoration onto the jug.

beaded slippers

These were found in a department store and just cried out for some embellishment. We used the holes in the fabric of the slippers to guide the sewing, making it very easy to do.

Materials

straw and hessian slippers
three colors of rocailles—¾ oz
  (20g) of each will be enough
black polyester thread

Equipment

dressmaker's pencil
needle
scissors

1 Draw your design onto the shoes.

2 Thread the needle and pick up your first bead. Go into a hole, back out of another hole and add another bead.

3 Change the colors as you progress, building up the pattern.

4 When you have finished working the design bring your needle back up the slipper, weaving it in and out a little. Then secure the thread into the underside of the slipper binding.

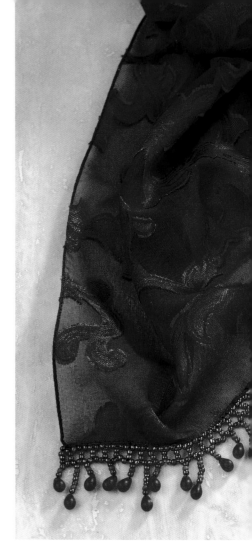

fringed scarf

An ordinary scarf can be made very special by adding beads to it. We picked beads of the same color as the scarf and wove them into a band for the ends, then added some luxurious fringing.

1 Start by making a band of honeycomb weave to go along the edge of your scarf. Leaving an end to your thread, pick up eight of the red rocailles and thread through the first four again, making a circle. Now pick up six more and thread through the last two rocailles on the first circle. Back through four on the new circle, add six more rocailles and again thread through two on the previous circle and four on the one you have just made. You should be creating a neat row of circles next to each other (see diagram on page 123).

Materials

black polyester thread
red 8/0 rocailles (3½ oz (100g) should be enough)
¾ oz (20g) pink rocailles in the same size
red drop beads

Equipment

fine needle
scissors

3 Now attach the band by sewing through the scarf and picking up the top two rocailles in each of the circles of the honeycomb weave.

2 Measure the row against the scarf to check that you have the correct length.

4 To make the fringing, thread through the bottom beads of the band. Add a few rocailles, including some of the pink ones, and one of the drop beads, then thread back up through the rocailles. The drop beads have their hole across the top, so they will hold each length of fringe in place. We have made the fringing in different lengths and small clusters along the scarf. Repeat all of this for the other end of the scarf.

evening bag

The addition of a stylish flower and a length of beading can make a shop-bought bag quite unique. The advantage of both additions is that they are complete in themselves, so you don't need to do a lot of sewing on the bag, which is rather stiff.

1 Cut 23½ in. (60cm) of the wire, thread through one bugle with two rocailles either side and move them to the center. Thread the same selection of beads again.

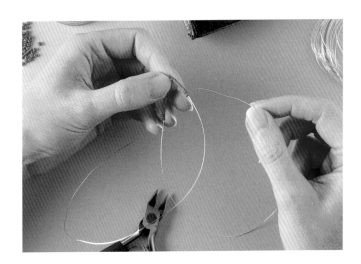

Materials

22 yards (20 meter) x 0.4 wire
⅓ oz (10g) red 2.5cm bugles
¾ oz (20g) red and purple 8/0
  rocailles
black polyester thread
silver fabric bag
1 central bead

Equipment

wire cutters
round nose pliers
flat nose pliers
small needle
scissors

2 Now bring the wire back through them from either side. You may need to use the flat nose pliers to draw the wire through.

3 Repeat steps 1 and 2 for the next row, but add another rocaille on either side of the bugle to increase the width of your shape.

4 Keep going until you have nine rows in a petal shape. Bend the ends of the wire around the sides of the shape to finish off and clip them neatly.

5 When you have made five of these pieces, cut another length of the wire and thread it through the bottom of all of them, drawing them into a circle.

6 To complete the shape, twist the ends of the wire together and wrap the loose ends back into the work.

7 The band for the top of the bag is made in flat gourd stitch. Place four rocailles onto a long thread, then add a rocaille and work back through the third one on the row before, add another and work back into the first, on the next row add a rocaille and work into the sixth bead, add another and work into the fifth (see diagram p123).

8 Continue in this way, changing the colors regularly, until the band is long enough for the bag.

9 Now attach the band of gourd stitch to the bag. Just catch tiny stitches into the bag and the band.

10 Sew the central bead for your flower onto the bag. Finally, sew the flower shape onto the bag, using a few stitches to secure it to the fabric.

terracotta pot

Your house plants may not be luxuriant, but you can make them look very stylish in these decorated pots. This project will give you an opportunity to practice your wiring skills and have the fun of selecting beads that fit in with your decor and look good with your plants. Remember that you can adapt these designs to the size of your pots and choose beads that are right for your room.

The blue pot was given one coat of vinyl matt emulsion paint, and was decorated with silver plate wire and a selection of coordinating beads. By adjusting the amounts of wire and number of beads used, you can decorate smaller or larger pots.

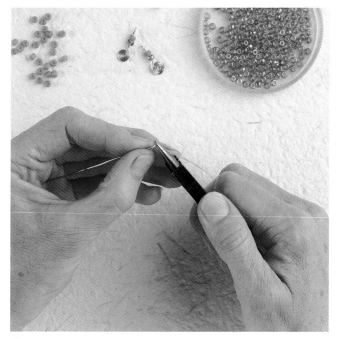

1 First make the small hanging pieces, beginning with the small coil. Cut 24 pieces of wire, each 3 in. (8cm) long. Using the round nose pliers, make a small loop at the end of one of these pieces.

Materials

13½ ft. (410cm) x 1.0 copper wire
29 small glass cube beads
102 x 6/0 shiny glass beads
30 x 6/0 matt glass beads
11 ceramic beads
6 medium sized Ghanaian powder glass beads
6 small Ghanaian powder glass beads
22 glass disc beads
1 terracotta pot, 6 in. (15 cm) in diameter

Equipment

wire cutters
round nose pliers
flat nose pliers

2 Lay the flat nose pliers across this small loop. Holding on to the wire firmly, use your fingers to move the rest of the wire around the loop to start to form a coil. Release the pliers from time to time to reposition the coil. Leave about ½ in. (15mm) of wire at the end of the coil then use your pliers to bend it into a right angle against the coil.

3 Slide a couple of small glass beads onto the wire above the coil, then use the round nose pliers to make a loop, at right angles to the coil, at the top of the piece of wire. Make sure that the loop is big enough to have a piece of the wire threaded through it. Make another 23 of these coils.

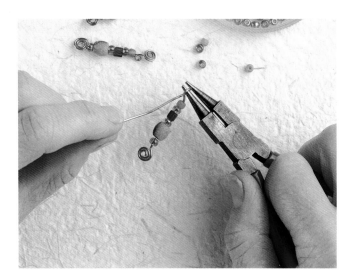

4 Next, make the long hanging pieces. Cut six pieces of wire 4¾ in. (12cm) long. Make a small coil at the end of the first piece and thread some beads over it. Then, holding the wire in the round nose pliers, wrap the wire around the tip to form a loop above the beads. This should be big enough to allow a piece of wire to be threaded through it.

5 Make a small loop at the top of the piece of wire and coil back down toward the beads to finish off. Make five more of these pieces.

6 Now make the hooks that will hold everything onto the pot. Cut six 7 in. (18cm) pieces of wire and make a coil at one end of the first piece. Thread one medium-sized powder glass bead above the coil, then make a loop in the wire as described in step 4. Now use the broadest part of the round nose pliers to form a curve. Once you have this shape, bend the wire around the rim of the pot. With this shape formed, make another coil in the end of the wire. Make five more of these pieces.

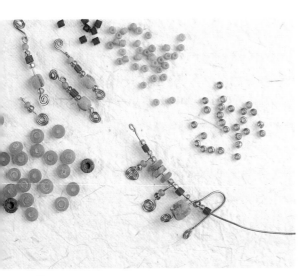

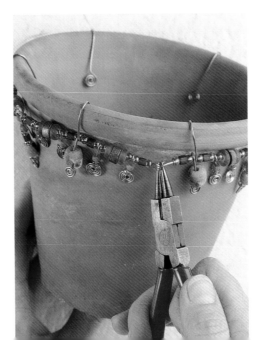

7 Cut a 19¾ in. (50cm) piece of wire to wrap around the pot. Make a loop at one end, then thread on all of the beads and hanging pieces following the pattern shown in the photograph. Make sure that all the loops and hooks point in the same direction so that the end result will be neat.

8 When all the elements have been threaded on, position the wire around the pot and push the hooks over the rim. Trim any excess from the end of the long piece of wire and make a little hook to go through the loop that you made at the beginning. This will complete the circle and hold everything securely in place.

Explanatory Diagrams

Buttonhole Stitch

Knot a new thread onto the thread or threads that you are working on. Make a loop in the new thread, then pass it around the core thread or threads and back through the loop. Draw the thread tight, then repeat until you have the required length of buttonhole stitch.

Overhand Knot

This knot is what most of us think of as a simple knot. Make a loop in your thread or threads, pass one end through the loop and draw it tight.

Half Knot

You will need two "working threads" and one or more core threads.

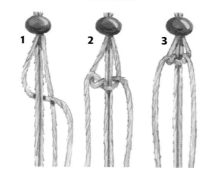

1 Move the left thread under the core threads and over the right thread, but don't pull it tight.

2 Take the right thread over the core threads and under the left thread (it will pass through the loop made with the left thread and the core threads).

3 Pull the threads a little to tighten the half knot, then repeat the process. Once you have completed four or five knots you should see that the knotted threads are forming an attractive spiral shape.

Square Knot

Like the Half Knot (above), you will need two "working threads" and one or more core threads.

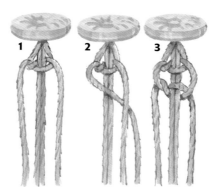

1 Move the left thread under the core threads and over the right thread. Then move the right thread over the core threads and under the left thread (it will pass through the loop made between the left thread and the core threads).

2 Now reverse the movement: put the left thread *over* the core threads and under the right thread.

3 Move the right thread *under* the core threads and over the left thread. Keep alternating these movements until you have the required length.

Securing Loops

1 Make a loop in the wire using round nose pliers in the position required.

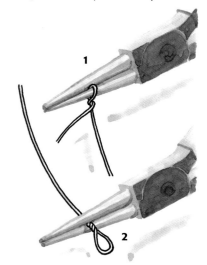

Make sure you leave a "tail." Hold the loop with your pliers, and with your fingers wrap the "tail" neatly around the wire a few times to make a coil.

2 Clip off the end of the "tail," and press the final coil with the pliers so the sharp end doesn't stick out.

Weaving on a Loom

Attach the warp threads to the loom.

1 With a comfortable amount of thread on the needle thread the required number of rocailles onto it, and pass the needle beneath the warp threads.

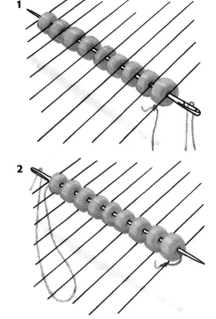

2 Hold the rocailles in place with your finger, then bring the needle and thread back through them but *above* the warp threads. Repeat for the next row and continue until you have the desired length.

Flat Gourd Stitch

Thread four beads onto the needle. Pull the thread through the beads, making sure you leave a long "tail." Thread on a fifth bead and pass your needle through the third bead. Thread on a sixth bead and pass your needle through the first bead. Thread on a seventh bead and

pass the needle through the sixth bead. Thread on an eighth bead and pass the needle through the fifth bead. Continue in this way.

Gourd Stitch

1 Thread the needle through three rocailles. Next thread the needle through a fourth rocaille and back through the first rocaille to make a circle. Thread on a fifth rocaille, and pass the needle back through the second rocaille.

2 Thread on a sixth rocaille, pass the needle back through the third rocaille and so on. If you want to increase the

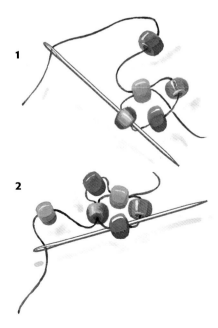

width of the tube you are making, add two rocailles before threading back through one on the previous row for one row, then continue as before.

Honeycomb Weave

1 Place eight rocailles onto the thread, leaving a long "tail." Pass the needle through the first four rocailles again to make a circle.

2 Thread a further 6 rocailles onto the needle. Pass the needle through the last two beads of the previous circle.

3 Pass the needle through the first four beads of the new circle again. Add another 6 rocailles and continue as above.

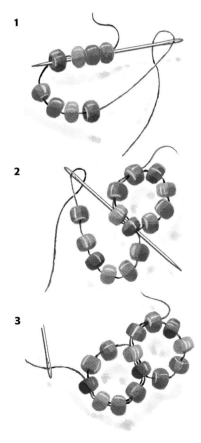

Index

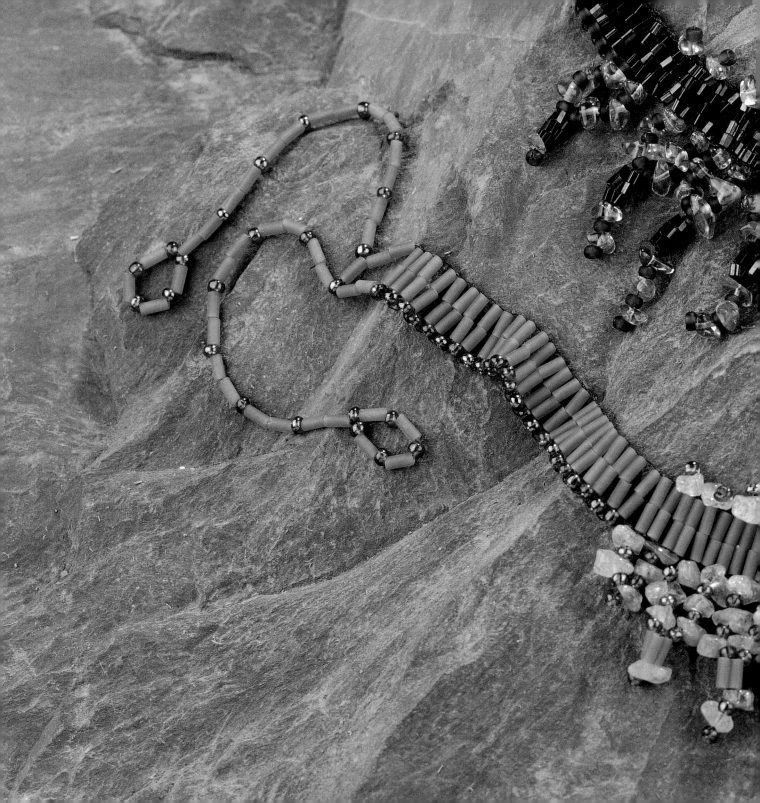